30 AND OUT

by Kit Sinclair

Published by Playdead Press 2023

© Kit Sinclair 2023

Kit Sinclair has asserted their rights under the Copyright, Design and Patents Act, 1988, to be identified as the author of this work.

A CIP catalogue record for this book is available from the British Library.

ISBN 978-1-915533-17-3

Caution

All rights whatsoever in this play are strictly reserved and application for performance should be sought through the author before rehearsals begin. No performance may be given unless a license has been obtained.

This book is sold subject to the condition that it shall not by way of trade or otherwise, be lent, resold, hired out, or otherwise circulated without the publisher's prior consent in any form of binding or cover other than that in which it is published and without a similar condition including this condition being imposed on the subsequent purchaser.

Playdead Press
www.playdeadpress.com

'*30 and Out*' opened at Pleasance London on May 30th, 2023. It then went on to do a four-week run at Pleasance, Edinburgh Fringe Festival 2023.

Creative Team:

Writer and Performer:	**Kit Sinclair**
Director:	**Charlotte Ive**
Producer and Dramaturg:	**Rebecca Prentice**
Movement Director:	**Lolo Brow**
Composer and Sound Designer:	**Nicola T. Chang**
Caption and Lighting Director:	**Rachel Sampley**
TSM / Operator:	**Roshan Conn**
	Han Sayles

Generously supported by Arts Council England and the Phoebe Waller-Bridge 'Keep It Fringe' bursary.

Kit Sinclair (She/He/They)

Kit Sinclair is a gender nonconforming multi-award-winning performer and writer. They recently won the international Nancy Dean Playwrighting award.

Acting credits include: *EastEnders, Casualty* (BBC); *Inspector Lewis* (ITV) and feature film *Giddy Stratospheres.*

As a writer Kit is currently under commission for Hampstead Theatre having been a part of their Inspire Program mentored by Roy Williams.

Kit was also on the Kiln Artists Development program and is a Soho Theatre Alumni writer.

Kit's previous play *'Gigi Star and Her Vocal Cords of Magic'* debuted at Applecart Arts after a sold-out run in 2022. Their solo show *'Awakening'* completed a highly successful run at the Underbelly, Edinburgh Fringe Festival where it was listed as a Lyn Gardner top pick.

Kit's short film *'Aeroplanes'* (directed by Cannes winner Paul Shammasian) screened at festivals worldwide including BAFTAs Underwire festival where Kit was nominated for 'Best Actor'.

They currently have three TV shows in development, two short films in pre-production, and a theatre show under commission with Prentice Productions.

Prentice Productions was established in 2022 by Rebecca Prentice with a focus on high-quality, form-blending, meaningful theatre and film.

Productions include '*Gigi Star and Her Vocal Cords of Magic*' which debuted at Applecart Arts in 2022. '*Mermaid*' which opened at Theatre 503 in 2023, and short film '*Driving with Tim*' featuring Simon Callow.

'*30 and Out*' is a piece that will forever be one of the most important and personal pieces of work that the company has made.

With special thanks to:

Jane Harrison and John Abbott | For continually believing in me, for seeing all of my shows and for helping me get to where I am today. Without you both, I wouldn't have discovered my purpose. Thanking you hardly touches the surface of my gratitude

Catriona, Peter, Fiona | For always supporting me. Forever seeing my work and being brutally honest especially when I don't want to hear it.

Denis Lawson & Karen Prentice Lawson | My new extended family (God help me)

Bryony Kimmings | Your autobiographical course opened my mind to endless creativity. Without your teachings and support this production wouldn't be what it is. Thank you, a million times over.

Carlo Constandinou | For saving my life more than a few times.

Bec Rodger | For believing in me even when I don't – Love you mate.

Hugo and Brett | For your endless support and our love language of queer memes.

Ella Platts | The bestest friend, neighbour and support angel I could ever ask for.

Estelle Bingham | For changing my life.

Chloe Burton | For the excellent production shots and filming.

Saskia O'Hara | For the brilliant poster.

Thank-you also to:

Yanou, Tringa, Adrianna, Jac, Michelle, Annisa, Elisha, Kate, Hannah, Clare, Catherine, Rocky – my group of angels. My amazing '*30 and Out*' team, Hannah Williams, Louise Ripley-Duggan, Theseus Agency, all the staff at Pleasance, everyone we interviewed, Arts Council England, Stonewall, Diva Magazine, Manchester 53Two, The Actors Pub, PlayDead Press, Apple Cart Arts and for every lesbian on this planet – this story is for you!

This production was interwoven with excerpts taken from interviews which were conducted with lesbians across the UK, as part of a wider archiving project to represent lesbian voices in 2023.

Whilst *'30 and Out'* draws from my personal journey of coming out aged thirty it was vital that this production also represented the wider community. Myself, and the Prentice Productions team, spent hours interviewing these amazing humans to find out how their coming out journeys contrasted and compared with my own.

This play would still work without the excepts but I feel they really make it something special, so I have included the sections we used in the original production in this publication.

Choosing the excepts featured was a nightmare! I wish we could have chosen more. Their voices and stories are extraordinary. I urge you to listen to them in full and to all the other amazing lesbian voices which didn't make this version of production.

They can all be heard in full at:

www.interviewsandout.com

For

Becca Prentice – My Fancy xx

The play is adaptable for any space, but the debut production was performed in thrust. The set sparse, nothing but a kitchen island and stool centre stage. A mic and stand behind a glitter curtain stage left, and a black umbrella stage right, also hidden by a glitter curtain.

Preshow music morphs into a Voice Over of Kit's voice, saying:

KIT V.O: If you had a choice, would you choose to be heterosexual or homosexual?

What does being lesbian mean to you?

A flurry of female and non-binary voices fills the space. Apart from the odd phrase, such as "I was eleven", "the heartbreak was bad", "community is everything" you can't make out much of what is said. The flurry reaches its peak before cutting dramatically and becomes a classic waltz style of music.

SCENE ONE: Housewife Cis-Life

Kit, dressed in non-descript trousers and a blouse, swans centre stage. Kit holds a pose, much like a Stepford wife, out to the audience. Robotic grin on face.

Over the music we hear a disturbing 1950s advert for a wife's behaviour in servitude to her husband whilst Kit begins to waltz, prepare a flower arrangement and decorate a cake with fruit.

The sound is interrupted by a moan as Kit distractedly caresses a flower. The moans intensify, Kit is trying to ignore them but is also increasingly drawn to the sensations of her fingers in the flowers and the smell of the fruit. The music and voiceover deteriorate until it is just a crescendo of orgasms. Kit fully succumbs to the flowers and the grapefruit – it's about as sexual as it can get!

By the end of the scene, Kit has mounted the table, her face fully in the fruit, the flowers fingered to destruction. She's lost in the divine pleasure of feasting.

The music cuts /

MALE VO: Honey I'm home.

KIT: I'm coming!

SCENE TWO: Bit Awkward...

Kit slowly dismounts and cleans themselves up, eyeballing the audience sheepishly before-

> Wow, you're all here. Witnessing my-... That's... Amazing.
>
> I'm Kit – or Kirsty, depending on which point in the journey we meet – and I've just blown up my entire life. You've all just seen me fuck a peach because apparently, I'm a le-
>
> Surprise! Who knew, not me.
>
> People often describe me as fearless, which sounds very risky... What it actually means is I do things without thinking.
>
> *That* fandango was my old life. I had a very lovely partner, a cis man, and we had a relationship for twelve years. Childhood sweethearts. Ethan was my- Kirsty and Ethan were –
>
> No point looking back, not got the time.
>
> Now, I've discovered this major part of my identity, it's time to start again. Sounds fun, right? ...Who doesn't love a second chance.
>
> Thing is, I haven't got a clue what I'm doing so it's important I prewarn you – this is going to get messy. Literally. It's going to look insane. There will be poetry, recorded voices, and if you're lucky a song and a dance.
>
> Spoiler alert, I've just turned thirty.

Yes, THIRTY. That's ten times three. Quick maths.

Three decades dedicated to being straight, but it's fine because I've figured out the problem. I can start living, I can come out now and it's going to be amazing! These are going to be the best years of my life!

Are you ready?

Great. Like I said, fearless. No point beating about the bush. Let's get to the bush...

A mobile phone pings. Kit smashes her hand into the cake and pulls out a phone covered in cream. She licks the cream off.

Oh. Got a match.

SCENE THREE: She's Burning Up

Kit's legs are spread. They hold their phone between their legs as if taking a photo of her vagina.

KIT: Darcy, I need your help.

DARCY: Jesus Christ, that is a very unique shade of red

> Got myself into a bit of a pickle so I've called Darcy, my only gay friend, for some moral support. Darcy hasn't seen a vagina since the day he came out of one. So, his advice feels a bit futile.

DARCY: I can't keep staring at it, Kit, it's making me feel sick.

> It feels like actual flames are radiating from between my thighs. Didn't have time for a wax, so I've used hair removal cream and now she's burning something chronic.

DARCY: Just have sex in the dark

KIT: What if I miss and go in the wrong hole?

DARCY: No such thing babes.

Darcy hangs up.

> I wasn't sure of the etiquette with pubic hair and queer sex. So, I did what I've always done. I took the whole lot off. I appear to have had quite a severe allergic reaction. This is not how I expected to lose my gay virginity

DATE: Is everything alright in there?

Fuck! I rifle through her bathroom cabinets. Aloe vera gel! I slather my bits in green gunk... Come on, come on, come on

SCENE FOUR: Deflower

Kit launches herself out of the bathroom into the boudoir of an experienced lesbian seductress, voiced by Nigella Lawson. Kit becomes a giggly teenage boy whilst trying to follow Nigella's suggestive instructions, failing to execute the moves with any precision or delicacy. It's up to the actor to find the physical representation to the following instructions. A degree of improv is required. The more ridiculous the better...

NIGELLA: Let me show you my aromatics
I derive great satisfaction
Which simply involves
Cream, vanilla, eggs,
Sugar, a sink full of water and a blowtorch
Then it's a case of just folding everything gently together
Okay, just shove that there
Which is where all the flavour resides
Just split it lengthways
Stick it into the wine
Just turn on the heat
Mmm yeah
I'm aiming for a regular circular shape
Which means a lot of flattening and smoothing
And turn the heat back on slightly higher if you like to live dangerously
You're eating this
Stir constantly
Having said constantly
For an hour and a half
Taste as you go along

              Cream whipped
              You want it lusciously thick but not stiff
              Gently fold in
              You don't need to do much of this
              Because the whole point is to have the smoothness of the cream rippled with the tart fruit
              You don't want this one pink homogenous mousse
              Mmm tastes like boiled sweets
              And the minute it goes in
              Mound, pleasurably –

Just as Kit finds her flow, the voiceover switches and Jane Fonda is yelling commands from a 1980s workout video. The suggestive miming becomes frenetic, nonsensical limbs flying everywhere.

JANE FONDA: Be sure you have a towel or a mat close by
                    Touch down and don't forget to breathe
                    Come up as high as you can on your toes
                    Go for the bird
                    Walk your hands back
                    Lunge to the left
                    Ensure your left heel is down and your elbow is pushing your knee up
                    This is the cardiovascular part of our workout
                    Legs side to side
                    Resist. Resist. Resist
                    Make it burn
                    With your upper arms parallel to the floor
                    8 now 8 and
                    Now legs apart
                    And scissor

>   One two three four
>   Lock the elbows
>   Now lock your fingers
>   Get it up
>   Now scissor
>   And up
>   Over the line
>   Inhale
>   Exhale shhhhh

NIGELLA: Right turn over

Finally, exhausted, it is Kit's turn. Legs spread waiting like a desperate pretzel out of breath but eager for their turn...

DATE: I don't do porno pubes.

Kit closes their legs, embarrassed. They look at the caption board. The following interview excerpts are projected onto the board in situ with their voices.

```
I was elated.
I was so happy.
And I'd been talking to a girl
online for, like, years-
two years maybe?
And we were always,
we'd meet up and kiss and…
But she was always in and
out of having boyfriends.

And then one night we
finally stayed over.

And I just remember laughing
the whole way through it.
```

It was quite,
it was quite innocent:
it was really sweet.

And I remember straight after,
I came on my period,
like, instantly.
And I remember I was wearing,
like, big, pink, fleecy,
heart pyjama bottoms.

There was, like,
no inhibitions.
it was quite sweet.
But I was just
so happy that I'd
lost my virginity.

> First, we took a bath
> to, like,
> see each other naked
> for the first time.
>
> But wh- I remember,
> when I saw her body,
> I was like,
> 'I am done.
> I am completely done'.
>
> I was just flabbergasted.
> I don't remember if we
> were even kissing
> in the bath
> to be honest.
>
> I think we were just
> getting comfortable with

                    being naked together.
                       Once we had sex,
                         we had sex for,
                  like, a week nonstop,
                          all the time,
                       many times a day
                                It was,
                    it was a crazy ride.
                          I, I, I could,
                    I would do it again.

           That sort of, like,
           bus pilgrimage to Lourdes?

           That was my first sort
             of lesbian encounter,
         sitting beside that person,
                like, maybe, like,
            touching their hand and
                    being like,
          'Oh! That's a big feeling'

We were drinking tea.
She got up,
stood against the wall.
I got up.
Next thing I knew,
I was snog-
we was kissing.
And then we ripped
each others' clothes off
and went to bed
and had the most amazing
mind-blowing sex
I've ever had in my life.

SCENE FIVE: I Guess I Should Know Now...

Kit lies quietly next to her date, now asleep.

> We lie under cheap polyester sheets.
> The femme fatale kimono
> She flaunted a few hours ago
> Lies crumpled round the leg of her bed
> Like any old tatty dressing gown.
>
> I don't know what I expected.
> Some sort of magical spell
> Or transformation in my cells
> But all I feel is disappointment.
>
> No different than I have for thirty years.
> No closer to understanding what it is to be-
>
> We blended skins
> Interlaced limbs
> I've finally felt the pulse of a woman
> Inside.
> Her power pressed against my palm
> My Sapphic innocence morphed into experience(ish)
>
> So where's the eureka moment?
> Shouldn't it burst like confetti;
> All heady yet steady in certainty?
>
> I squirm in the night's silence.
> Perhaps I can escape unscathed'
>
> I shimmy down the bed.
> She pulls my arm across her chest
> Forcing me to cocoon her.

No escape.
As the arch from her spine fuses into my torso
We meld into a human half- moon crescent.
As the curve of her thigh melts into mine
And just like that, all my discontent lessens.

This is the sign I've been seeking!
Like two puzzle pieces
We jigsaw together
Slotting next to each other like it was always meant to be.

I've never held a woman before.
There are no sharp angles, no jagged limbs which feel at odds
This moment just changed the landscape of my existence.

This is it.

SCENE SIX: Too Desperate?

> Shut her front door, strut down the street – I'm a new woman. Bloody legend.
>
> Do I look different? If you didn't know, would you be able to tell?
>
> I race up the stairs, two at a time, slam the key into my door and head straight to the bathroom mirror to see –

Kit stares ahead as if staring in a mirror trying to see a difference

> Oh...

Kit feels something behind her ear. She pulls it out and examines it.

> The back of her earring... I should return it. No, too keen. She'll think I'm desperate. I want to keep it like a memento. Put it in a tiny glass jar - An ode to the lady who took my virginity.
>
> Yeah, no that's just weird.

Kit looks at her hair line. She gasps

> No... Silver threads shimmer like the start of a spider's web

SCENE SEVEN: Funeral for Straight Life

In order to fully embrace my new life, I should honour the last thirty years with a proper send-off.

Kit pops open an umbrella. Sound of rain. Sombre atmosphere.

VICAR: Ashes to ashes. Dust to dust. For thirty years, Kirsty gave her all to the tradition and culture that makes society what it is today: heterosexuality. With that in mind, let us say our goodbyes to that which was thrust upon her and which will no longer be a part of her world.

Goodbye...
All Bar One
Live, laugh, love
Penis straws at hen dos
Ed Sheeran
Gender reveal parties which cause forest fires
Holidays in the Maldives, Dubai, Russia, Poland, Qatar, Malaysia, Tennessee
Having a biological child with your partner
Feeling safe kissing in public.

The follow interview excerpts are heard and projected:

```
I just went to see a movie
with a person I was seeing
at the time.
And there was two men
sitting behind us,
and one of them booted,
like, really hard
```

this person's chair?
Like, just, I think she
just kissed me on
the cheek or something.
He, like,
volleyed her chair.
And I remember really
being like,
'Wow! This is, like,
blatant homophobia'.

    My actual first, direct,
        um, sort of
     homophobia comment
     was when I was on
  holiday in Turkey actually.
    Um. And I went with
      my partner and,
     well my ex-partner,
      hehe, and, um,
      we was getting
    sort of looks left,
    right, and center,
   and sort of whispers.
It was definitely something
very rude and, um, hurtful,
    and it just made me
  feel very uncomfortable,
    as soon as I entered
    the country really,
     and then every,
  the customs was even
   being really funny
 because it was obvious
    that I was gay,

and my partner didn't
look like she was,
so I think they put
two and two together,
and then –

We decided to move
in terms of having a
better future together
because, um, in Poland,
we are not able
to get married still.
And still, like,
the government doesn't recognise
same-sex marriages,
or, generally,
same-sex relationships.
So, that's the main
reason why actually
we decided to move-to have,
like, a better future together.

SCENE EIGHT: Let's Get Educated

> I get educated. I watch seasons one through to six of The L Word; A problematic show, but it's all there is. It is my bible. Everything's slotting into place perfectly.
>
> I've slept with a woman.

Ding

> I've embraced the culture.

Ding.

> I've bought a pair of Doc Martens

Ding!

> All these things should empower me enough to say, 'Hi, I'm a l-...'
>
> It wants to explode out my being,
> But some how it's disagreeing with my mouth.
> Like water and oil unable to blend,
> This word has festered foul in my gums.
> Its syllables unable to wrap around my tongue
> Without conjuring:
> Exclusion
> Biphobic
> Transphobic
> I so want to claim this word as my own but how can I when it ferments in a quagmire of hateful rhetoric...

The following interview sections cut in:

> Like I think I probably
> heard the word lesbian,
> usually in a bad way.
> Like, some girls might say,
> like, 'Oh, she's a lesbian,'
> meaning, like,
> she's probably a bit,
> like, like,
> butch-presenting
> or something.
> Or like, or even like,
> she's not very pretty.

> I think I've been on
> a real journey,
> actually, with the word les-

> It's like –
> if you've got issues
> with it yourself,
> how can you
> expect other people,
> how can you challenge,
> you know,
> those negative stereotypes
> and stuff?

> It was always,
> like,
> the crazy aunt
> who was an alcoholic
> and does drugs
> is the lesbian...

> I think 'lesbian'
> is particularly difficult
> in our, in our –
> I love it –
> but whenever I'm talking,
> just before I'm
> about to say it,
> there's a bit of a pause?
> Because it just feels,
> like, depending on
> what rooms you're in,
> it's a bit of a bomb
> you can drop
> that just makes people –
> Menopause is the same weirdly.
> Growing up,
> and particularly
> being in high school,
> being called a lezzo,
> if you like,
> was the worst thing,
> you know the worst
> kind of slur or –

Yet amongst the debris it still shines bright luring me in. I skirt around it, fearful of its downfall- or power - time will tell. Either way I'm not ready for the repercussions. So, I say:

Hi, I'm a homo, a gay woman, a queer, part of the LGBTQ+ community, a tribadic-

Kit stops, looks at 'tribadic' projected on the caption board....

Really?

The definition of tribadic appears on the caption board:

N. Archaic. *A woman who rubs herself against another woman for sexual pleasure; a lesbian.*

> Oh well, yes, I've done that – once. The average person in their thirties has had nineteen sexual partners. Time to get smutty.
>
> It's no secret that the gays know how to party... Feed me to the hounds!

Kit slips on a pair of white gloves...

SCENE NINE: Pulse with Pride

Lights and music ramp up.

> I've convinced Darcy to accompany me to a lesbian night. Turns out lesbian clubs are hard to find. Hours of research to discover sweet fuck all. Anyway, here we are, outside a one-off night in a sweaty hotel basement.
>
> I didn't know what to wear so I've gone hard on the 'fancy dress is encouraged'

They gesture to their gloves.

> I'm a French mime. Darcy's Aphrodite – We look like we're sponsored by Poundland.
>
> The butch security guard pats me down before –

Beat

> Is she not going to let me in?
>
> My hand, shaking like a baby's rattle, thrusts my decade old driver's license into her stony face. I want to scream it's real. I'm gearing myself up to explain this isn't my first rodeo! Despite it very much being my first rodeo.

BIG SUE: I'm Big Sue, any problems come find me. I'll be on the door all night.

> Problems? A room full of women surely means solutions. Big Sue gives me the dyke nod of approval

Big Sue does the dyke nod.

> And we're through the door.

DARCY: You rolling yet, babes?

Darcy's pupils are the size of eight balls. I haven't touched MDMA since I was sixteen.

DARCY: What you waiting for?

He has a point... I look around, hoping I'll know when I see it.

Kit takes some MDMA. The music swirls and crescendos.

HOLLLLLLLLLLLY SHIT that feels good! The dance floor floods with butches in leather and femmes towering in heels and non-binary beauties in harnesses, someone's wearing fairy wings, there are biceps and boots and sports bras.

Sound of women screaming.

DARCY: These bitches are bursting my ear drums! Is this what a girl's boarding school sounds like? Collective screaming to shit pop music?

It's exhilarating, it's terrifying, it's everything I didn't know I wanted! Everyone's really good looking. Are gay people just infinitely hotter?

My stomach; a mass of butterflies.
My knickers – soaked through.

KIT: Darcy! I feel amazing!!! What a brilliant night!

DARCY: It's the drugs babe, this is fucking awful. Smoking area. Now.

They're now in the smoking area.

> I'm bumper to bumper with beautiful women. Darcy's swamped. My six-foot four hairy bear chested Aphrodite towers like a skyscraper. I've never seen him look so scared. Lesbian energy is magnetic. It's powerful, unapologetic.
> Aesthetically everyone looks like they've stumbled out of Berghain.
> I am on cloud nine! But jeez do I feel out of place.
> I try to re-enact what I saw on the cover of Vogue.
> I strike a pose under the smoking sign.
> Where I lean like James Dean against the railing.
> Aloof... but really, I need the support.
> My feet feel like they're filled with helium and I'm about to buckle under this palpable queer power.

SMOKING GIRL: Hey you... Got a light?

> Does she mean me?

DARCY: Give her a light, Kit

KIT: I don't have one...

> Darcy snatches a lighter out of a spotty teenager's hand.
> Is everyone here twenty-one?

SMOKING GIRL: I've not seen you before

KIT: I've only just come out!

SMOKING GIRL: From where?

KIT: The closet!

SMOKING GIRL: You what? Hey... We love a bit of FRESH MEAT here.

Like hawks preying, dozens of bloodthirsty eyes scan me – I feel validated. I feel a million bucks.

SMOKING GIRL: How old are you?

KIT: Thirty

SMOKING GIRL: For real? Wow. Most people your age don't bother

This hits hard. Kit reacts as if they've taken a blow to the stomach. A cacophony of voices repeats 'most people your age don't bother' heartbeat sound throbs underneath. It peaks before cutting abruptly –

DARCY: It's almost three, let's go babe

Who does he think I am? Cinderella? I couldn't care less. I've never been happier! I feel safe. Unleashing my sexuality amongst glitter cannons and glistening sweat. I'm living my best gay life!

I waltz through the crowd pumped with pride when I see Her... She summons me. The crowd parts like the sea. My legs glide towards her, I am Jesus...

SCENE TEN: A Million Things

I roll out the club high on drugs, and love, frankly – what's the difference? Darcy's nowhere in sight. It's just me and Her.

Neither of us ready to part ways. We perch outside a bus stop for hours. Chatting shit. Her skin feels electric. I'm too high to make out half of what she's saying, but it sounds cool. She's interesting – I think.

ME: Do you want to come back to mine?

Bold as brass – Who even am I? She's thinking about it... She's –

HER: I do. Very much, but I'm a gentleman so I'll wait 'til your bus comes and then arrange a proper date.

Smooth. We wait. Limbs sprawled over each other like strands of silly string. I want to ask her a million things, but my bus is here.

I watch dawn break from the top deck of an empty bus. Feet on the window bar I stare endlessly at her WhatsApp picture – face half concealed with her phone, but it's enough. I just met the love of my life. My future wife.

I doom scroll BBC news with a grin the size of England slapped across my face. Nothing on this shitty planet can pierce my high. Ears still pumping with Tegan and Sara. Pride still pulsing through my veins when –

Pulse, Orlando Florida. 49 murdered in a club identical to one I was just at.

I don't understand... But I felt so safe, so free... My mind replays the night. I think of Big Sue, the girl in the smoking area, the butches in leather, of Her

Kit steps forward

If our own clubs aren't safe, where are we supposed to go?

The caption board projects the following statements. Kit reads them

9 people sentenced after acid attack outside famous Dalston queer nightclub 2019.

Club Q, Colorado Springs, 5 dead, 2022.

The number 49 counts up to 54 on the board.

That is fifty-four dead

Kit lights a candle. This is now a vigil.

I'm sorry I don't have enough candles. Every time someone is murdered from the queer community our souls shudder. Their trauma imprints on our own. We all feel it. Every time Big Sue pats me down at the door, I hold my breath, think of them, and pray we all get to pulse another day.

Kit takes a deep breath and stares straight ahead.

Kit holds her breath until she can't anymore. As she gasps for air the candle blows out. The number 54 evaporates on the screen.

Back on the bus, now chock-a-block wall to ceiling with briefcases and penguins in grey suits. I stumble down the narrow stairs, clutching the yellow railing for dear life. I can't breathe – MDMA mixes with grief. A grief I've never had to experience. I can't breathe- Let me off. LET ME OFF!

The below interview cuts in:

```
        There's been a,
       there's been a few.
        Um. I, I'm kind of
           thick-skinned,
    so the, the little comments
        I, I kind of brush off,
           but there's been
        a couple of occasions
     where, um, I've been out,
          and I remember one
         particular occasion,
         um, this male tried
         to make some advances
            at me and, um,
     I was kind of very polite
           and said, 'No'.
              I was at,
           we were actually
             in a gay bar
              at the time,
          which somehow makes
            it a lot worse.
    Um, uh, we were in the,
         in the smoking area,
       and he was very adamant
          about getting with me
             and touching me
```

             and, um,
        I had to kind of keep
            saying no, um.
        He got very frustrated
          and grabbed my hand
    and burnt me with a cigarette,
         and I still have kind of
            a little scar on my
              hand from that.
            Um. So I rememb-,
        I remember that happening.
        Um. That one really sticks
             out and… I don't,
          I don't even know how
             I, how I felt about
               it at the time.
             I jus… Obviously,
       incredibly upset. I rememb-

SCENE ELEVEN: Dyke Dripping DNA

That first club night fumble turns into the hottest summer of my life!
Think heat chasing pavements, crop tops, Adidas shorts.
A season of hazy, blazey roll ups and rose quartz crystals
Pressed against sun kissed skin.

We swim in hedonistic debauchery.
Park days roll into sleepless nights
I am the innocent in her arms,
I realise I've never loved anyone before
12 years with Ethan didn't even scratch the surface

She holds court and fame in a world I long to be in.
Her name trickles through a scene I can only access when I am an accessory on her arm.
I bask in her lesbian anecdotes
Eager to absorb by osmosis.

She has Dyke Dripping DNA
I am putty in her hands.
I replay her carefully curated 'Hello Sweetheart".
Said in a manner only a lesbian can.
The way she runs her hands through my hair sends shivers down my spine.

It's like she realigns every bone in my being
Then dislodges them again just because she can.
And I let her, every time.
I fall hard and I fall fast.

She doesn't.

The following interview sections cut in:

                    I don't know,
              I kind of wish that
                  I had just been
                   broken up with,
                   like, a month in
              and then could have
             been upset about it
              and then moved on
                       type thing.
                         But no,
                    they were all,
               like, disgustingly
                    strown out of,
                    strewn out of,
                even, of, like,
                  sending letters
              and being mushy-gushy,
           emotional stuff of, like,
          'Oh, but If we change this…
                      If we do this…
                         Oh my god.
               It was such a ballache.
                        Just move on!'

I am actually having
my heart broken
right now
to be honest…

               It was like someone
                had put a dagger
                through my chest.
                     Just like,

'Ah, the pain!'.
I could never love
a man like that.

Yeah, I think my
first girlfriend
broke my heart, but –

Especially after,
you know, I,
I put my lover in a box
and made myself
forget her.
I had dreadful
mental health.
While I recognise that,
yeah, this system
and patriarchy
and all that is
a large part
of the reason why
my children are here,
my children are a large
part of the reason
I'm still here.

SCENE TWELVE: Where the Divorcées at?

DARCY: You look horrendous. Eat something you silly cow.

KIT: I can't Darcy, I'm bereft.

DARCY: Just fuck someone else.

He clearly doesn't understand the complexity and nuance of lesbian love. I can't just carry on.

KIT: Most people my age my don't bother

DARCY: Get back on Hinge – now

KIT: All single women in their thirties have either no chat, or they've ghosted me.

DARCY: Then lower the age to less than twenty-five-

KIT: Absolutely not

DARCY: You'll be waiting for the first round of divorcées to come through.

I increase, and decrease, the age bracket, pay off my monthly mortgage and set up a pension- Anything to not think about Her.

SCENE THIRTEEN: How to Spot a Lesbian.

Kit walks on stage with a Ukulele… She sings the following:

> I can't play guitar but here I am
> With a ukulele- It's the size of my hands!
> Its time teach you all in my solo band
> How to spot a lesbian.
>
> They'll probably like cats, and own a few
> Look out for a Doc Marten platform shoe
> Expect a white vest, and lots of stamina
> Turns out that scent was just Lynx Africa – oh –
> How to spot a lesbian.
>
> They'll have short nails, at least two.
> If they're really talented, maybe a few.
> Sexy arms with lots of tattoos – meow –
> How to spot a lesbian.
>
> History says we never existed
> Religion makes us sound proper twisted
> I looked really hard at G-A-Y
> But it's been occupied by the straights since Ninety-Five
> I dunno where to spot a lesbian.
>
> They'll have long fingers, don't y'know
> I see you there, in the front row
> Copping a look
> You, dirty lesbian.
>
> I could go on all day with these subtle signs
> But I suggest you learn to read between the lines
> Cuz society still got us marginalized
> I guess it's hard to spot a lesbian

SCENE FOURTEEN: Good Girl, Gone Bad.

> She's blocked me. Says, "We can't keep doing that lesbian thing of talking for hours, saying we still love each other when we've broken up. It's not helping you move on... You'll thank me later."
>
> I won't. Fucking Bitch.

Kit performs a strip tease. They take in the audience, hunting for prey before ripping open their shirt to reveal a black sports bra and a leather harness.

She slicks back her hair then rips off her trousers to reveal tight black shorts.

Our good girl has gone fully bad. It looks like Sandy at the end of Greece just moved to Berlin and is living her best Berghain life.

A choreographed club scene follows – it's the opposite of the first scene. Kit flirts outrageously with audience members. Dripping in confidence. This is pure sex, pure filth, pure queer dark lesbian joy.

> I relied on her to access the queer world.
> Well, not anymore.
> There's a new lesbian in town
> And that lesbian is me.
> That's right- I'm owning it.
> The word trickles off my tongue like greeting an old familiar friend.
>
> **LESBIAN!!!!**

Strobe lights kick in and Kit begins to feast. A full-on club fuelled sex frenzy as she demolishes a platter of fruit. Peaches, figs, oranges, grapefruits. Kit squeezes fruit juices all over herself.

It's a hedonistic gorging frenzy - the fruit the women she's feasting on. It's the counterpart to the opening. The tone and sense now charged, dark, adult. This time Kit is in control of her sexuality and she isn't wasting any time...

As the strobe lights and music peak, we cut dramatically to the following interviews:

>   I feel like it was probably
>   the threesome that
>   I had with two other
>   girls on my
>   eighteenth birthday.

> She sent me a
> message saying,
> 'Hey, Sexy Stuff
> Let me know when you're home.'
> It was my husband's number.
> I was so drunk that
> I gave her his number.
> A lot of the people that,
> you know, you'd seen me
> say hi to, like, that was,
> there was a sex party
> the week before.

>   When that, when that
>   beat drops and the
>   music comes on,
>   I want, I want to

     be getting down
on the floor, dancing.
    You can't do that
    in your stilettos.

SCENE FIFTEEN: Heterosteria

> I hike up Primrose Hill towards three bobbing balloons. J & A.

KIT: Darcy!

DARCY: I'm sucking a train driver off in fifteen. What d'you want?

KIT: Abby and Jason's engagement picnic. Please tell me you're here

DARCY: I wasn't invited

> Darcy and I set them up. Course he's invited. He's being dramatic.

DARCY: D'you what. Fuck 'em… I don't go where I'm not wanted

He hangs up

> I edge closer towards the metallic balloons glinting in the sun, blinding me.
>
> Arriving early wasn't an option but being late is… Humiliating.

ABBY: Kirsty!

KIT: Hi Abby. It's Kit now

ABBY: Right. Of course! Kit's here everyone. Oh, I'm so glad you could make it.

KIT: Hey guys

ABBY: So, we have news... Jason got us a puppy!

KIT: Oh my god, where?!

ABBY: Oh! Prim isn't ready to be socialised yet

KIT: Sounds like me

Awkward beat

ABBY: You look so different...

A row of couples in pastel dresses and chino shorts stare up at me. Several fingers freshly decorated with diamonds.

ABBY: You must have been so anxious coming alone, but don't worry, Ethan's in Malaysia with his new girlfriend, not that it matters, because you will always have invite-priority.

KIT: Thanks.

ABBY: Come sit next to me and Jas. Tell us all about your fabulous gay life. Looks like you're having a ball... Are you loving it?

The following interview sections cut in:

```
Because in Poland,
I ca-, I was taking
part in Pride,
it was all about,
you know, fighting
and the fight
for the rights.
And here, I felt
```

that it was both
fighting but it
was also so normal
that it was also
like a celebration,

                I think sometimes
         you don't even necessarily
           realise that you're
     holding bits of yourself in.
        Even me who, you know,
          I will often introduce
           myself as, you know,
            a black gay woman
             in my 40s, just
because… Or even like Black Pride –
            that's when I feel
        probably most comfortable
        in that sort of setting.

        And they are nights
        and they're, they're
        about drinking and
       they're about dancing.
        And I love drinking
          and dancing.
      But that's not everything
        the community is.

So, I really struggle
being in really noisy,
alcohol – And also
those spaces often really
sex-oriented.

And it's just
not always,
like, where my head
is at or what I'm needing.

SCENE SIXTEEN: PRIDE!

Kit spins round wrapping themselves in a pride flag. 'It's Raining Men' blares.

> IT'S PRIDE BABY!!!!
>
> Every gay's second birthday. I've been counting down the days until my first Pride, and it's finally arrived! And I get to attend with a date. They're edgy, different. They instruct me to stay away from the rainbows and to wear all black

Kit dramatically removes the rainbow flag. She stares at her all black outfit

> Sorted. We stomp through Soho. United. Proud. I dodge the gazes of girls I never called back. Their lustful eyes linger. That's right, soak us in. My partner is smoking hot and dripping in queer nonchalance.

THEM: God, another year getting crushed in Soho Square.

KIT: It's amazing, right?

THEM: I fucking hate this capitalist shit.

Kit makes a disagreeing face...

KIT: Same

> I can't believe I've missed out on all this! The crowds burst like a skittles rainbow, and I am ready to taste the joy. Two leather daddies in buttless chaps sander past. An appalled parent covers his children's eyes. Someone from a Qatar Airways stand thrusts a mini flag in my

face. Everyone stares at my date – Back off bitches, they're mine. We're all sun soaked and tipsy. A fabulous silver fox also dressed head to toe in black blue steels us:

Air kisses

SILVER FOX: Fashion darlings! Wouldn't be caught dead in rainbows, we're far too cool.

Queer kinship and I am here for it. Forget pastel chinos and engagement puppies, give me fashionistas and leather pups!

SILVER FOX: Erm, blue eyes... Where's your boyfriend? Surely he hasn't left you alone with a bunch of raging homosexuals. How uncivilised...

KIT: My boyfriend?

I point at my partner who thinks this is hysterical

SILVER FOX: Oh! OH... You really can't tell nowadays can you.

It hits Kit hard, but she tries to brush it off.

Not important, is it. I don't need to look to belong...

SCENE SEVENTEEN: Everyone I Date is...

Kit picks up the Ukulele

> I don't mean to sound sentimental...

She starts to strum and sings the following...

> But I'm hoping the next will have potential
> My Pride date was a bit temperamental
> I'm sure that it was purely accidental
> When they stabbed me in the leg with an eyebrow pencil.
>
> I'm hoping the next will have potential
> Turns out this one's a tad experimental
> Got carried away with a kitchen utensil
> Oh! I think I prefer things a little more gentle
>
> I'm hoping the next will have potential
> I've found someone who's really environmental
> Got me on a diet of eating only lentils
> But every time I'm naked she's really judgemental
>
> Now I feel like I'm losing my potential
> These gays are giving me existential
> I'm exhausted
> But society says at thirty I should settle...
> So you understand why having a partner feels pretty essential

She dramatically strums an open cord in an emo manner.

SCENE EIGHTEEN: Partner in Chaos

KIT: Darcy, let's get out and get fucked up

DARCY: Kinda done with all that babes, sick of being used and consumed – Too old for that shit

KIT: You're twenty-five

DARCY: Exactly. I'm into real intimacy now. Did I tell you, I'm seeing someone. A Taurus. You should see the size of his hands, he's like a fucking bear.

Darcy doesn't *date*. This is good actually, really good. Darcy deserves this and it's an opportunity for me to find my community. I don't need a relationship. I need my people.

I join a Lesbian Book Club. I am dyslexic, I survive two weeks.

I try queer football. I'm never picked to play and they're all dating each other.

I learn to roller-skate. COVID means we have our weekly skates on Zoom, my downstairs neighbours complain.

But it's fine, because these are going to be the Best Years of my Life. Even if so far they've been –... Just gotta try harder.

The following interviews cut in:

> But I have really
> good friends that have
> been with me since
> the day I came back
> from Italy to London
> and came out.
> Since then, we've been
> the same people,
> you know, pretty much,
> and it's, it's
> just really great.

I think it, like,
it can only
be beneficial,
as early as possible,
for people that are
queer to be around
loads of other
queer people.

> Because all of my
> friends are pretty
> much party animals.
> So we see each other
> every week because
> we always go out.
> As a queer woman,
> there aren't
> many spaces.
> I mean, when I say that,
> there is one
> bar in London.

Like, it's She Bar
or nothing.
I get to meet a
lot of people
and it's always
the same people
because we are
all so hungry for
events that are
for women loving women
and that feel safe.

SCENE NINETEEN: GAME OVER

Kit pops an imaginary coin into an imaginary arcade game. We hear the coin jangle before the sounds of a school video game fire up. Kit takes up a fight position and bobs in rhythm. She is now the main player in this fight. The following statements fly onto the caption board, she interacts which one. It's up to the actor to decide which statements win verse which ones Kit wins.

GAME V.O: You should be settling down by now
IVF average cost = £6,000 – £8,000
Mr & Mrs
Who wears the trousers in the relationship?
You just haven't met the right man
You're too pretty to be a lesbian
My second cousin is gay. You should meet them
I'll pray for you
But how do lesbians have sex?

The game eventually defeats Kit.

GAME V.O: GAME OVER!

Fighter Kit deflates as the game powers down.

SCENE TWENTY: Domestic Bliss

> Everyone loves the honeymoon phase. Endless hot, sweaty sex. Oh! So thrilling but seeing as everyone else has settled down, it's time I do too.
>
> 'Actively seeking commitment: No time wasters please'

Kit brings on an imagery partner. A small movement sequence follows, to show Kit and their partner in flow. Everything is working out perfectly. They're sharing, preparing and it's smooth sailing. They waltz together, an homage to 1950s bliss, before setting in for dinner. Kit throws a tablecloth over the island.

> Welcome to domestic bliss.

Kit pulls their partner's seat out, then tucks them in.

> The love bubble that is our past five months has kept us afloat, buoyed us up nicely.
>
> I've made their favourite meal for the millionth time.

Kit clears the plates away

> The foggy sex mist stage has cleared and I'm praying they still want to continue life with me.

Kit turns around to their partner who has clearly left. Kit deflates briefly before...

> Sometimes you've gotta kiss a few frogs. Then dust yourself down and get back on the horse.

Kit presents partner two. The same movement sequence is repeated, with subtle changes. Perhaps this partner is smaller, or they don't flow as smoothly, maybe they stand on each other's toes etc. They're trying to present as happy clappy but it's tense. Through gritted teeth:

> Why are you yelling at me? Will you just- Stop. You're acting like it's all my fucking fault...

Partner two disappears.

> Like I said, frogs until you get your princess.

Kit jumps onto action. She's ready and waiting for partner three to arrive. She holds a pose summoning them. Kit waits an uncomfortably long amount of time.
She waits some more.
She checks her watch.
She scratches her bum.
Kit breaks the hold, shakes out her leg.

> She's not usually this late.

Kit jumps back into the hold with more vigour! Kit's willing them to arrive... She waits, and waits, and waits some more until accepting that she's late.

> She works shifts. Probably been held up

Kit holds onto her last bit of hope until...

> Frogs.

Kit removes the tablecloth.

> I'm sorry, but I just can't do this anymore.

Kit sniffs three lines of cocaine.

SCENE TWENTY-ONE: A Bit Gay

Kit sits at the island. Now a bar table. Terrible generic bar music plays. Think 'All Bar One' vibes. She's on a date.

MAN:	Not going to return the compliment then.
KIT:	Sorry. You look like your photos too. Well done.
MAN:	You're acting a bit like I've forced you here.
KIT:	Sorry, I'm just keen for this to stay a one off
MAN:	I was only setting the mood.
KIT:	That's fair

Kit's body language suggests he puts his hand on her knee. He goes in for a kiss. She's clearly a bit awkward

MAN:	I'm not doing this. You should leave
KIT:	I'm literally offering sex, no strings attached
MAN:	Yeah, I'm not into what you are

Kit is taken aback. Shocked, then impressed.

KIT:	Oh my god, is it finally that obvious?
MAN:	I'm not like most men
KIT:	…
MAN:	I like experienced women
KIT:	Do you think I'm a virgin?

MAN: I'm an Atheist

KIT: What do you think I'm offering here because it's not the bible

MAN: I've met girls like you before and I'm not being fooled. Again.

KIT: Listen, I've slept with men but I'm a lesbian and women are actually a bit too intense actually. The heartbreak is so painful. I feel so lonely. I don't fit anywhere. My life is running out and I miss human touch. And I just thought, maybe, sex with a man might give me something.

MAN: Fuck

KIT: I didn't expect to be accused of being frigid and using Hinge to sell religion. So cheers mate

MAN: D'you want another drink?

KIT: Yes, yes, I do. Very much.

Kit downs another drink.

MAN: Everyone is a bit gay nowadays, aren't they

KIT: Are they?

MAN: Yeah! I'm not, but I think it's pretty cool. Homophobia is bullshit

KIT: Yeah, it is

MAN: It's pretty sexy, actually. I love lesbians. I mean, I'd be down for that – Next time you should bring one of your friends. A little Minge a trois, eh.

The following interviews cut in:

```
       I actually prayed really hard
                - you know my little
              self prayed really hard
                    to wake up and be
                    attracted to boys
```

```
She invited me to have
conversion therapy
with her and I was
really torn because,
you don't want to
go to Hell for eternity,
and she was the
second person to offer me
conversion therapy
and the first
was a psychiatrist...
```

```
     I think it would be
      really superficial or
         shallow to say I
       wouldn't change being
    queer for anything, because
     that queerness comes with
           the struggle and
            I don't love the
     internalised shame I have.
        I don't love that...
```

I never thought I'd
live to be thirty,
I didn't think I'd
live to be twenty.

SCENE TWENTY-TWO: I Hold My Breath

Kit is outside the club.

> It's not ideal, but it's all I know. This is all I've got. Big Sue's on the door – Guaranteed free entry. There's four ahead of me.

Whispers of 'Most people your age don't bother' are heard. Just like the voices in the club earlier on. They swirl and swarm. Kit tries to ignore it, but they increase until she's shouting over them.

> Come on! I can't stay out here. I've been out here for too long! As I reach the top of the queue, I do what has now become tradition, a superstition, four nights a week I hold my breath for all those who never got to pulse another day.

Kit takes a big inbreath. Just like before with Pulse. As she gasps the captions, lights, and sounds all CUT abruptly. A short, sharp blackout.

SCENE TWENTY-THREE: She's Got Me Cornered.

The Lights flick up. Ugly strip, exposed lighting. Kit sits on an upside-down cardboard box. She looks at the audience.

> You're all still here then? Watching me fall apart. Just me and Big Sue locked in a stockroom under this deeply unflattering light.

BIG SUE: How the fuck did you end up here, Kit?

KIT: You dragged me in here, Sue

BIG SUE: You gonna tell me why you're acting like a maniac? Why you whipping up a storm like a spoiled toddler in a sweet shop?

A fair but unnecessary comparison.

BIG SUE: You ain't right in the head, love. This ain't who you are

KIT: You don't know who I am

BIG SUE: Well, that makes both of us then.

KIT: Ouch... I lost thirty years of my life not knowing I was gay.

BIG SUE: Who says they were lost?

She's got me cornered.

KIT: Apparently most people my age don't bother coming out, and I get why now. There's no manual. No one teaches you how to be a gay. When I came out, I unearthed this massive part of who I am, but in doing so I've lost myself. I feel like I don't belong anywhere.

BIG SUE: Hold on, rewind... You telling me you're worth less 'cuz you've come out late?

KIT: Yeah

BIG SUE: I've got three kids with my ex Harry. You saying I'm a lesser lesbian cuz I was married to a man for twenty years?

What? Big Sue is old school butch through and through. There's no way she was ever in the closet. Her gaze makes it clear she isn't joking.

KIT: I can't stop thinking about all the relationships, the connections I've missed. I feel like a teenager falling in love for the first time with all the wrong people

BIG SUE: Is being in a relationship how you validate your gayness?

Oof. Talk about a low blow.

BIG SUE: Just because you haven't got it all sorted doesn't make you a bad lesbian, Kit. Just makes you human.

KIT: I thought being gay was rainbows and queer joy, but it's so painful.

BIG SUE: You telling me none of it's been good?

KIT: Some of it's been great but a lot of it's been awful.

BIG SUE: That's life sugar tits

KIT: Everyone from my old life is hitting massive milestones

BIG SUE: You've come out, I'd say that's one massive milestone.

KIT: I just want the chaos to stop

BIG SUE: Alright. Kit, you're banned from the club.

KIT: What?! That sticky, sweaty basement bar is the only key I have into any ounce of community.

BIG SUE: You ain't gonna find yourself on that dancefloor, love. Go home. Figure out who you are when ain't getting used or consuming the first person who shows a sliver of interest.

Kit removes the harness, and in slow motion puts on a plain tee. The following voice overs boom and project onto the captions board. A sense of time pausing

BBC NEWS: Boris Johnson has just announced that England will enter another period of lockdown.

ABBY V.O: So, Jason and I got married. Erm, obviously totes would have invited you. It just there really wasn't space... Hope you're thriving!

BBC NEWS: A lesbian couple were brutally attack on a London bus near Camden on Saturday evening.

DARCY V.O: Babes, I've just seen your ex kissing that girl you've been hanging out with. Ain't she your new mate? Bit savage to be honest

BECCA V.O: Hey, it's Becca from work xx

SCENE TWENTY-FOUR: Rainbows and Unicorns

So, this is the bit where I show you how I got my life together. There should be glitter cannons, rainbows and unicorns... But I promised to be honest. After Big Sue banned me, I spun out some more until I just didn't have it in me.

I was tired. Really tired. The world isn't set up for being queer. How you navigate your entire life changes. Is this space safe? Will that person judge me? Being gay is wonderful but it's exhausting. So, I gifted myself the one thing I didn't think I had- Time.

I took time out. From dating, from clubs, from everyone apart from Darcy. Not very dramatically pleasing, I know. It was much more fun when I was fucking the fruit, right?

D'you know what, thank fuck for Big Sue. Her tough love saved my life, and it got me thinking; Who was Big Sue's Big Sue? Who did she talk to? On that note, I couldn't not give you a happy ending. Two years ago, I had a one-night stand and in true lesbian fashion it never ended.

I'd like to introduce you all to my fiancée Becca, she's operating the captions now...

The caption board spells out: **Hello!**

She's made it all worthwhile... It's cheesy, I know. I'm Becca's first lesbian partner. Going through all this has meant I was able to hold space for her as she went through all the ups and downs I did. I've sort of been her Big Sue…

Becca and I will get married.
The 'Don't Say Gay' bill is only an Ocean away
So, I'll say 'I do' because one day
I might be forced to say, 'I can't'.

I felt a lot of embarrassment about coming out late, so in an attempt to heal that I interviewed lesbians all over the country to find out how their stories compare to mine.

A voice recording of Kit asks the following questions. Just like we heard at the beginning of the show

KIT V.O: If you had a choice, would you choose to be heterosexual or homosexual?

I've lived two lives. I know which is easier, but I have to be me. I am a rainbow flag bursting with joy, where the fabric is woven by fingers which hold centuries of trauma, shame and pain. Colours stitched together by HIV positive blood, forbidden sweat and lonely tears.

KIT V.O: What does being a lesbian mean to you?

How is anyone supposed to answer that? For me, to be a lesbian means to be happy, but it also means to be different. And difference breeds fear. And it's accelerating…

Brexit unleashed a tidal wave of hate
So venomous you can taste acid leaking like old batteries from the letters of the Daily Mail.

Homophobia is up thirty percent.
Transphobia is up seventy.
Why did we become the enemy?

Section 28 may be dismantled
But trans people are getting trampled
I've never felt threatened by a trans woman in a bathroom
So, whether it's abseiling in parliament or marching in the streets
For me, to be a lesbian means to stand up and fight for those who need allies

I'm speaking up because if not now, when?

If not us, who?

So yeah, being a lesbian to me means all that, I guess. Plus, I'm not just a lesbian. I'm a gender non-conforming lesbian which is a fancy way of saying nonbinary.

Kit lets it sink in...

Does this mean I have to come out all over again?

THE END